Princess CHINNI Goes to School

Isabella Dipesh

BLUE PENCIL

About the author

I am Isabella and I am twelve years old. I live in Hyderabad and study in Meridian School. My father is a management consultant and my mother is a consultant Acupuncturist and a Naturopathist. As a child, I loved to read books (which I still do!) and share stories with my parents.

Growing up, I began writing short stories for my little brother. The hobby turned into a fierce passion for me. My first story 'The Magnet That Attracted Girls' has been published in the anthology Ocean Blue by Scholastic.

When I'm not writing or dreaming up stories, I love to play jazz tunes on my piano, cook for my family, do artwork and read G.K. in my free time. People often call me nerdy, but I would say, I'm curious to learn more. I remember how thrilled I was when I first learned to read, to be able to access the many worlds of fiction. My mission is to hold children spellbound with my stories and to evoke in them a love of reading.

I also want to help save the environment in little ways such as recycling, composting and planting trees in my backyard. I'm not sure what profession I'll take when I grow up, but one thing's for sure, I want to be an author who travels around the world, collecting tales of different cultures, and be the change I wish to see in the world!

My favourite quote that I thought of by myself is, "I would rather be an imperfect human than a perfect inhuman."

PRINCESS CHINNI GOES TO SCHOOL

Isabella Dipesh

First published by Blue Pencil 2021

BLUE PENCIL

A Venture of Wisitech InfoSolutions Pvt Ltd
76/2, 3rd Floor, East of Kailash, New Delhi - 110065
Ph: + 91.95828.49600
Email: sales@bluepencilpublishers.com
www.bluepencilpublishers.com

Edition 1

ISBN: 978-81-952978-7-0

Cover Design and Illustrations - Blue Pencil Studio

Acknowledgment

I'd like to thank my parents, my aunt and uncle and my little brother for their endless support and encouragement. I'd also like to thank all my teachers for inspiring me and teaching me to express myself in different ways. I want to thank all the prayers warriors who keep praying for me and encouraging me. I'm ever grateful to everyone at Blue Pencil, especially Antara ma'am, who worked on editing this book and made it the masterpiece it is now. And above all, I would like to thank God without whom I would never be who I am today.

"I can do all things through
Christ who strengthens me"
- Philippians 4:13

Contents

Chapter 1

Welcome to the Palace

It is a bright and sunny day. Princess Chinni wakes up in her lovely canopy bed, decked with ornately carved bedposts and silk bed sheets with floral prints kept neatly at the end of the bed. The bedsheets are made from imported silks which traders have acquired after travelling many countries and bargaining hard. Her golden spaniel gives her a big sloppy lick for her to know it's time to start the day!

She is awakened by the call of the peacocks that are bred in the palace gardens. She glances around her room which is as big as a mansion. Her eyes fall on her toy cupboard. She slowly walks to the cupboard and her golden spaniel, whose name is Daniel the Golden Spaniel follows her. She flings the doors open with a dramatic air and looks up to see thousands and thousands of costly plush toys, dolls and beautiful figurines.

Princess Chinni rings her servant bell. Soon she is surrounded by hordes and hordes of servants, wearing their red and white chequered aprons and bringing fresh flowers from the garden to adorn her hair. Some help her get dressed and change her lovely nighttime brown pyjamas and comb her fine sheet of jet black hair and some clean her room.

She soon finds out that she is going to be visiting the villas where her father works. She quickly puts on her lovely pink frock which has dainty little frills on it and her pretty little tiara which is topped with a matching pink jewel which lights up her tanned, sober, little face that makes her look really nice. She runs out of the palace and is greeted by the neighing of her coach's horses and the beaming smile of her kind coachman. She hurries inside the coach and instructs the coachman about the destination, who immediately turns around and beams at her.

"Would you be a dear and get me to the villas where my father is holding a party, please?" the Princess asks the coachman. Without further ado the coachman drives up straight to her father's party. When she reaches there, she hears a loud call. After a few minutes she is awake.

***

Chinni realised she had fallen asleep in the sandpit. "It is not real. It is not true. It is just fake! It is just phony," she cried out with tears hot in her eyes. She was thoroughly disappointed. The castle and the maids were made of sand and sticks. The coach and the coachman were just bugs. Her father really did work at the villa site, but as a construction worker. Her tiara was made out of vines and her pyjamas were rags. Her lovely gown was a rag too. She was just a simple villager girl.

Chapter 2
Reality Strikes!

She was truly disappointed, but that didn't stop her from imagining she was royalty. She went inside her shanty house and pretended it was a bungalow. She went to the dining area, which was actually a dirt rag to sit on and eat. She told her sweet mother Latha, "Give me some food to eat! You should have served it for me much earlier! If you keep up at this rate, I shall have to whip you." She spoke as if her mother was a maid.

"Dear, dear! What has gotten into you? First of all, I am unhappy because my salary for this month hasn't been paid and now, you go all high and mighty and order me about as if I am your drudge," Latha said.

Hot tears swelled up in Chinni's eyes. She ran to her favourite tree - which was a mango tree, sat dejectedly beside it and cried for almost an hour. "Why, why has God put me in this state? While he could have put me in the palace, I've to stay here and weep in the pit. Curse the princesses who live a royal life. Oh God!" she thought.

"Chinni, Chinni, where are you, Thalli?" she heard her mother shout. She put her face into her cupped hands and refused to show it so as to say, "Leave me alone, Ma." Her father

Srinivasa came right at that moment, and called out, "I have come home, Chinni darling. Where is my nice little dotty?"

"This Chinni is angry with me," said Latha.

They waited till evening but still Chinni didn't come out of her little hiding place. Soon it was time for her parents to go to work again, and so they went leaving Chinni to cry to herself.

Latha was hard at work, washing the vessels and making the house spic and span, but the employers would still not have it. They would shout at her if a single spot of dirt was found, they would scold her and insult her by saying she was a big lazy fool who didn't know a thing.

Srinivasa's state was even worse. Day in and day out, he would have to carry heavy bricks, handle sticky mortar, and stand in the sun for the whole day. They wouldn't give him a day off, not a second's rest, even on Sundays.

Fun Activity

Search on the internet about International Labour Day and help out your parents and maids by giving them a day off in a year to make them feel nice.

You can do things like:

1. Help wash dishes
2. Help water plants
3. Help old people with their stuff
4. Help clean things and tidy up
5. Help fold the washed clothes.

Chapter 3

Technological Advancements in the World

The world was changing. There were metro trains which were driverless. Skyscrapers and highrise buildings were having their glass panes cleaned by robots. As Latha peeped out from the window, she saw robots sweeping the streets. She wasn't shrewd so she foolishly called her employers and showed them the sight. "At least they are more accurate than you are!" her employer Raagini, the mistress of the house, sneered at her. "The day after tomorrow you shall be fired," said Raagini. "Before you came we had already planned and made arrangements to buy these special robots which are meticulous, unlike you. They are impeccable," she continued.

Latha was heartbroken. She ran home, sat in

an empty corner of her shack and cried.

Chinni walked in and saw her mother crying and sobbing like a small child. She felt sad for her mother when she heard about why she was crying. She ran out to the garden and quickly made a small bouquet with marigold, Latha's favourite flower. Latha soon cheered up with the fragrance of the lovely flowers and more so because of the love shown by her daughter.

Latha stayed up late that night. She thought of a plan to stay hired. At 5 in the morning, she went to her employer's house. The robots had been delivered to their doorstep by the creators of those efficient machines. She did not know much about technology, but she knew if she twisted any button, the robots would stop working. So she set about removing the robots packaging, pressing all the buttons. By the time the rooster crowed, she was already back at her house, pretending to be asleep.

Soon, when she thought that her mistress and master would be awake, she ran to their house. As she went inside, she saw her employers were frantically testing the robots and because of haphazard pressing of the buttons, the robots were saying, "Maids are Idiots." Luckily she didn't understand what they were saying.

Raagini saw that their maid had entered the house. She told her husband to switch on the robot and at once it started saying, "Maids are idiots, robots rule! Yeah!" Raagini translated the robot's words to Latha in a simpler language in which she would understand. Latha gasped in horror and she thought, "My own trick has rebelled against me. Does the world like me anymore?" She certainly was furious at herself.

The whole day she was not able to concentrate on her work because the robots were beeping here and there which made her make mistakes. She forgot to clean the cobwebs from the ceiling. She forgot to clean a big cupboard filled with dust. By the end of the day she was exhausted. Not because she had to finish the work but because of the robots teasing her around.

Srinivasa's situation was something similar. He was told he would be fired three days from now.

"Why am I to be fired?" he asked the contractor.

"We don't need construction workers anymore," said the contractor. "Instead, we got these amazing excavators, cement mixers, skid steers and wood chippers. We don't need any lazy old construction workers like you. Instead we got these amazing auto programmed machines, which is why you are being fired. It's a waste of money, paying wages to you, you know." And on that short note, he walked away, leaving Srinivasa to pick up his problems. The circumstances looked grim!

When the night came it was time for Chinni's parents to come home. Chinni noticed her usually joyful parents were as gloomy as dead men. No matter how much Chinni tried to cheer her parents up they wouldn't pay attention at all and so this made Chinni cross. Before sleeping, Latha and Srinivasa wished on a shooting star that they would get their jobs back.

The next morning time passed slowly for Chinni's family. Chinni had gone outside to play. In the afternoon they surprisingly found out that they were rehired! At first they thought that it was the shooting star that made their wish come true but seeing Chinni's mysterious smile they understood that there was something was fishy.

After a lot of cajoling, they found out from Chinni that in the morning, when she said she was going out to play, she had actually gone to both the bosses. She had shed copious tears and pleaded her parent's case. The bosses had felt sorry for Chinni and agreed to rehire her parents. Chinni's parents joyously cuddled Chinni after she told her tale.

Fun Activity

Do an interview with one of your grandparents to find out more about the differences in the world they grew up then and the world they see today and how advanced technology has become now.

You can include questions like:

1. Tell me 5 things that are common now but weren't available then.
2. What was your means of communication and transport then?
3. Are the means of transport and communication now better? Why?
4. If you wanted to send a written message, how would it be done then?
5. In what way are community services different now from the services in their times?

Chapter 4

Chinni's Toys

Latha got back from work holding a brown carton full of toys that her mistress gifted her, especially for Chinni to play with. She was welcomed with shouts of happiness by Chinni on seeing the toys that were going to be hers. The contents of the box were a toy train, a toy dump truck, a toy excavator, a few baby dolls and... a toy gun.

She slowly opened the carton and picked up one toy after the other, eyeing each one carefully. The toy train was red and blue with its bright yellow wheels that went "chug-chug-chug-chug" whenever they were moved. Her toy dump truck was bright yellow and black with a cute red STOP sign. You could put sand in it and dump it out. The excavator was yellow and black like the dump truck with its big, flexible, arm and bucket ready to scoop up the dirt and dump into the dump truck.

Chinni had seen these giant machines at her father's construction site and was fascinated to see their miniature versions. Chinni opened up the baby dolls and counted them. Each one of them wore a different coloured dress. One wore a red dress with a matching hair band to hold back her soft black hair and red shoes. The second doll wore a yellow dress with a matching hair band and yellow shoes. The third doll wore a white swimming costume and swimming gear instead of accessories.

Chinni never noticed the gun. She went off to play with her new toys and left the gun behind in the carton. Srinivasa soon came back from work and saw the carton. Assuming that it was for him he opened it and found the toy gun inside and the label that read 'CHARITY TOYS' and understood that it was meant for Chinni to play with.

Chinni saw the gun, before her dad could hide it and said, "Can I play with that?"

Her dad replied, "No. Haven't you heard of terrorist attacks before? Well, it all starts with this toy gun."

Chinni had no idea what her father's conversation was leading to. "How can a toy ever be related to terrorist attacks? What are you talking about?" said Chinni.

"Chinni, my little princess, you are too naive to ever understand these things. However, you need to know this. Well, it first starts when the child plays with such toys of aggression. These toys breed feelings of violence and hatred in the heart. The same feeling that starts a war and the tendency to shoot or destroy. Once you get feelings of hatred, there is no getting rid of them," her father said wisely.

"Oh, Daddy, you could be a peacemaker for the entire universe, you indeed are a wise father!" cried out Chinni and hugged him tight.

"Now, come and see how I play with my toys, Daddy!" Chinni invited her father. Srinivasa hurried along, being pulled and tugged on by

Chinni. They soon reached the place where Chinni was playing.

"Why are you not playing with your construction vehicles and train?" asked Srinivasa, seeing that Chinni had neatly separated her construction vehicles and train from her baby dolls.

Chinni had been to her dad's construction site before and had seen that all the vehicles were being manoeuvred by men not women and so, by this theory, she sorted those items and smartly replied to her father, "Because Daddy

they are boys' toys and I am not a boy."

Her father once again wisely replied, "There is no such thing as boys' toys and girls' toys. Both are equal. It is all in the mind."

"Then why do girls always play with kitchen sets and boys with machines and vehicles?" questioned Chinni.

"This is the conditioning given by the society we live in, my little girl. We expect women to be limited to the kitchen and men to go out in the fields and roads and become rugged. But, the world has progressed very far. This is the age where women are going to space and exploring the unreached ends. I wish we could someday afford to send you to a good school and make you explore the world around in a better way," Srinivasa said, wistfully. Chinni was again so proud of her wise father. Latha, who had been listening to this conversation from the kitchen, was brimming with joy.

Author's note

A gentle toy will always be better than a violent one. Toys can influence you and they should not be compared on the basis of gender. Choose your toys wisely. And also the cartoons you watch. They aren't just entertainment; they are your influence and they can make or break your future.

Chapter 5
It's Lunch time

It's lunch time!

"Chinni, O Chinni...where are you? Come on, let's make lunch," said Chinni's mom.

"Coming Amma," Chinni ran inside the home, putting aside her toys.

Chinni helped her mom peel the green peas which her dad had brought from the Rythu Bazaar. The Rythu Bazaar or Santha as they call it in local language, had a spread of all varieties of freshly procured fruits and vegetables from the farmers called "Rythu" in the local Telugu language. Spread across miles, this bazaar had a variety of fresh farm procured produce in myriad colours, sizes and shapes. It was a treat to the eyes to see these fruits and vegetables arranged in rows in this market. People flocked to this bazaar with their cloth bags and bought the choicest of fruits and vegetables. More interesting was the bargaining they had with the sellers. Chinni's dad would visit this place once in a couple of days to bring home the fresh produce.

While Chinni was peeling the peas, her father too joined in to help her. Chinni said, "Daddy, these are the chores of the ladies, why are you coming in?"

Chinni's father smiled and replied, "Chinni, there is nothing in which a man should not help. After all, like there is no such thing like boys' toys and girls' toys, there is nothing called 'only girls work'."

"Boys should be trained to help their parents, be it related to peeling the potatoes or fixing the nuts and bolts," he added. Chinni hugged her father in adoration.

Chinni's mom collected the peeled peas from them and offered to make aloo matar ki sabji (peas and potato curry) to go with the rotis.

Chinni's mom reached out for a dabba full of wheat flour and scooped out a heapful of flour onto a plate. She added a pinch of salt and sugar to it and a teaspoon full of oil to it, then she added half a glass of water to it. "Chinni, you can do your favourite activity now," said her mother.

"Yes Amma, I know exactly what to do," Chinni jumped onto her task. She washed her hands clean and sat down to knead the flour.

"Amma, isn't this the same flour we got ground at a small shop at Chintal Basti, my favourite basti?"

"Yes, it is called a ghirni, which is also called a flour mill. Milling is the process by which wheat is ground into flour. In our childhood, people used to grind or pound the wheat between the stones. They used the mortar and pestle or a saddle stone, which were all operated by hand. Now, you know why your grandmother has strong muscles, it is because she used her hands to do all the manual work to grind the wheat and make it as flour. But, now, they use metal rollers to grind the wheat and make it into flour," explained Chinni's mom.

"Quite interesting!" exclaimed Chinni.

"Yes, everything is changed now. Most of the work that people used to do manually is now replaced by machines and people are growing weak as there isn't much physical activity," said her mother.

"But Mummy, machines can't make rotis as tasty as you can and my tummy is craving for your yummy food," said Chinni. Her mother smiled and grabbed the kneaded flour to make hot rotis for everyone.

Author's note

Our muscles build up when we work. There is no such rule that only girls should do household work and boys should do adventurous and productive things and earn money for their hard work. Think about the mothers who do the hardest jobs of all, to feed, nurture, take care, cook and clean for the entire household? What do they earn in the end? Of course, they earn our love and respect and they deserve it.

But when parents tell their children to do some chores, the children give some excuse or the other and avoid their tasks. Eventually, the parents end up doing all the chores.

So remember,

Always do your chores,

Girl or boy it's all the same,

Work hard, don't be lame.

Chapter 6
Sustainability

"Reduce, Reuse, Recycle," is just as important today as when the phrase was first being used.

Even though Chinni and her family were very poor, they lived a sustainable life in spite of their low income and resources.

One day Chinni was playing with some pots and pans and was making music with them. She opened her kitchen cupboard where all the utensils were stored. As she opened up the pots and pans, she heard a little crack sound. She decided to investigate the matter and she soon found out that the handle of one of the pans was broken. She quickly ran to the repair centre in her favourite Chintal basti. There were pots and pans hung on the wall as display items. They were screws and screwdrivers of all sizes scattered on the table.

"Good afternoon Mr. Venkateshwar garu," said Chinni.

"Good afternoon thalli, how can I help you today?" said the shopkeeper.

There was a magnifying glass hanging from his neck, just to help him take a closer look at the screws and pins as he assembled things. Chinni brought out the pan from her sack bag, extended it towards him and said, "Can you please fix the handle of my pan?"

"Sure, I am good with fixing things," he said proudly and took a closer look at it with his magnifying glass. "This handle needs some glue and some screws to keep it in place," he said. He got onto the job and in a minute, it was done.

"Here it is, thalli," he said and handed it over to Chinni. She gave him a few coins and thanked him, tucked the pan back into the sack bag and headed home.

Chinni could not afford to buy a new pan, hence there was no option but to get it repaired. This is how she did her little bit to help Mother Nature and reduce waste.

As Chinni headed home from the basti, she saw her father cycling back home from his work site. She waved at him excitedly and jumped onto the pillion seat of the bicycle. A few turns of the wheels later, the cycle gave up. Shwooosshhhhh, the air went out from the rear tyre.

"Oh no," said Srinivasa. "This tyre needs another first aid."

"What kind of a first aid does the tyre need Daddy?" Chinni asked, almost amazed.

"Come, let us go to the nearest tyres and puncture shop, Chinni," said Srinivasa. Chinni was excited that she would get to see another kind of repair centre the same day and learn about the "first aid" for the bicycle.

"Hello Hussainji, how are you doing today?" said Srinivasa to Mr. Hussain who was busy mending other tyres and tubes. Chinni glanced through his makeshift shop along the footpath pavement, with a roof that was made up of green plastic sheet. On the wall,

this time, she found a new set of equipment that is used to mend the cycles and tyres. The tools were quite different from those she had seen at Mr. Venkateshwar's shop - spanners, hammers, tyre levers, wrench, axle, nuts of all sizes; patch kits, air pump and some old tubes. Mr Hussain took a break from his work at the tubes and greeted Chinni's father.

"Oh, I am good. Please tell me, how can I help you today," said Mr. Hussain. "The tyre has given up again and I need your magical hands to do the jadoo," said Srinivasa.

"Certainly, let me take a close look at it. First we need to pull the tyre out from the wheel," said Mr. Hussain as he used some tools to put out the wheel's rim and then pull the tyre out. He asked Chinni if she could spot any hole in the tube. Chinni inspected the tube which lay lifeless on the ground and said, "No, I cannot spot any hole. Can you, Uncle Hussain?

Mr. Hussain smiled charmingly and said, "I cannot spot with my naked eyes, but I have a certain kind of test which can help us."

"What is it?" asked Chinni with her eyes filled with curiosity.

"Come on here, beti." Mr. Hussain, took her to a tub filled with water and dipped the tube into the water pool and kept rotating the tube little by little in the water.

"Bubbles, bubbles," screamed Chinni excitedly.

"Bingo! That is exactly the litmus test. We found the hole from where the bubbles are emerging."

"Wow, I love this experiment," said Chinni. Mr. Hussain grabbed a patch of rubber from another old tube he had and took the patch kit and the super glue and glued it onto the top of the hole. He aligned the tyre back onto the wheel and filled the air with his air pump. The tyre was now mended. Srinivasa thanked Mr. Hussain and handed over Rs.10 to him and they both headed home on the bicycle.

Srinivasa was a superhero, who was contributing to reducing the carbon footprint in the world quietly. He went everywhere on his bicycle. No petrol, no pollution, no obesity!

They reached home and found Latha washing the clothes and hanging them on a rope, both ends tied to the two trees in their front yard. She had just a few sarees given to her by Raagini every year and she cherished them. Few of the old sarees she made into curtains for their little room and few other cotton sarees she used as a bedcover for the makeshift mattress they slept on.

Srinivasa too had just a couple of shirts and if a button was broken, he sure knew his life skills. Every boy and girl needs to be taught at a very young age to do the basic stitching. Chinni too knew how to stitch patches on her torn frocks. They didn't have many clothes, but they had just enough for their needs. There was no wastage.

Once Chinni's mom had finished washing the clothes, she poured out the used water from the buckets to the trees and plants outside their home, the art of recycling! They surely didn't waste an ounce of water, as they had to fetch water from a source far away from their home and they kept the buckets filled for the needs of the day.

It was already sunset. The moment they entered the room it was pitch dark inside and they could not see a single thing present in the room. So instead of switching on the tube light and using expensive electricity, they used a simple lantern to light up the room. They used electricity sparingly.

Author's Note

Every time, we purchase a product, do you know it has an environmental footprint? Starting right from the raw materials that are used to produce it to the gases emitted during manufacturing to the packaging which ends up as a non-biodegradable waste in landfills - all these count in the environmental impact. So before we buy anything, we need to question ourselves, if we really do need it.

Reduce, Reuse, Recycle, is the mantra of this era. Nothing can replace it if we need to save our earth and our lives.

You can car pool or use the school bus for commuting to work or school and do your bit to reduce carbon emissions.

Use cloth bags to carry the groceries and other shopping items. Never ever use plastic bags. Plastic bags and bottles we use in our daily life take 500 or more years to decompose. Stop buying packaged mineral water. Always carry your water from home in a steel bottle.

Chapter 7
Trees Make the World

One day Chinni woke up to the sweet singing of the cuckoo on her window. She got out of bed and headed towards the community tap to clean her teeth and wash herself clean. This was the common wash place for the people of her basti. Children would have a great time early in the morning brushing their teeth and taking bath together, more of a community bonding time.

After she finished, she ran back to the house to see what was for breakfast. To her delight, she found out that there was fluffy idli for breakfast and piping hot sambhar to go with it as well. Latha cooked sambhar with a lot of vegetables which made it extra special. Yummm!!! Chinni thought. She relished her breakfast and ate enough to fill 100 sumo wrestlers' stomachs!!

After she finished her breakfast she went out to play on her favourite tree branches.

She arrived at the spot and decided to scale right up the tree and sit on its comforting branches and listen to the peaceful sound of its swaying and feel the gentle rocking of the tree. She carried an old megaphone she had found with her so that her voice could be heard from above if needed.

As it was summer, the tree was full of ripe, juicy, yellow mangoes, ready to be eaten. Chinni, full of temptation to pick the most ripened, juicy and yellow mango, reached out her hand and the moment she tenderly plucked the mango, she heard a roaring sound. No, not a lion or a wild beast, it was the roaring of a much more terrifying thing. She spun around and saw the wood chipper! The big, scary machine was advancing towards the tree. Chinni let out a shrill, deafening scream which had three intentions:

1. to scare the wood-chipper-driver so he would stop

2. to start an action of protest against tree cutting

3. to alert her tree-loving, basti-folk of the maniac who wanted to cut down her beloved tree

Chinni decided that her basti-folk would never be able to hear her voice. But Chinni did have an exceedingly shrill voice. So just like a snake charmer uses his flute to charm a snake into doing something, Chinni decided that she would use her voice to stop the wood chipper-driver from cutting the tree! She purposefully sang into the megaphone in a way that sounded like an awful, unbearable shriek.

Soon the voice of Chinni became so intolerable that the wood chipper-driver ran away and was never to be seen after the incident. Chinni ran straight home and told all the basti-folk how she had saved the tree.

"And there I was singing for my dear life and the life of my dearest tree and finally the enemy, that is the driver, ran away in agony and was never to be seen again," Chinni

concluded. She exaggerated her story by swaying her hands to show her sorrow. She was quite an actress!

From then, Chinni and her friends always used that very same wood chipper as their secret hideout and her friends would remember Chinni's story and give her three cheers and a salute to the-girl-who-saved-the-favourite-tree – a title given to Chinni by the Sarpanch of the mandal for saving their healthiest, most beautiful looking tree.

Author's note

Trees take in all the carbon dioxide and give you pure and clean 100% oxygen that you breathe every day and to survive.

Why do you think there is a rising heat wave every summer and floods that wash away regions when it rains heavily? All because we are chopping away the life guards (trees)

Don't cut trees, don't cut the 'GUARDIANS OF LIFE.'

As a famous Chinese proverb goes - "The best time to plant a tree was twenty years ago. The second best time is now."

Sow a seed, plant a sapling and save a tree.

Fun Activity

Here are some gardening tips for you:

To ensure a healthy home for your seed you must make sure it has the three elements: water, air, sunshine. You also need to make sure it has the right pot size and the right potting mixture.

For the best potting mix - take cocopeat, compost and soil in 1:1:1 ratio and mix it properly. Add a teaspoon of neem powder to prevent it from pest attack and transfer the mix to a pot. Sow a seed or plant a sapling into the pot.

You can also try singing/talking to your plant for its good growth. Gardening can be an engaging and motivating hobby for you. Imagine, if you grow your own food, you don't need to buy the ones from the market which are loaded with chemicals and pesticides. I have learnt all this from my mom who is an expert at growing food for the family.

Go Green, Grow Green and never be Mean to the Greens.

Chapter 8

Education At Last!

One day, suddenly out of the blue came a Lamborghini car and it stopped exactly in the middle of the basti. Screech... the sound came. And from inside that car, a tall man stepped out carrying various posters and the picture of a palace.

"Mr. Thomas, why are you here?" Srinivasa asked, recognising the tall man as the architect he used to work for.

"I am here for advertising purposes and also to meet your little daughter as I have heard from you that she has high imagination." Mr. Thomas had heard how Chinni had saved the jobs of her parents and also the tree.

Srinivasa led Mr. Thomas to his little hut and to his daughter. "Hello dear girl! I am here to show you something," said Mr. Thomas. He looked quite grandiose to Chinni, and she kept looking at him.

And he showed the posters to Chinni. "This is a school called The Grand School of Excellence," Mr. Thomas explained. "It looks like a palace but it is actually a school for children as old as you."

Then Mr. Thomas asked, "Dear girl, would you like to see The Grand School of Excellence yourself? And perhaps if you like it then, would you like to get yourself an admission

form to the school?"

"Dear sir," Chinni replied. "It was always my dream to be the 'Princess of the Palace' and I see God is fulfilling the desires of my heart. It would be my pleasure and honour to join your palace-school indeed!"

So the trio (Mr. Thomas, Srinivasa and Chinni) proceeded to Latha to ask her decision towards the idea of Chinni going to school.

"Whaaaaaat! You want my daughter, Chinni, to go to school and study? You've gone mad or what, want my daughter to die?" She overreacted.

"Amma, first of all do you know what the words 'school' and 'study' mean?" Chinni asked her mother.

"Of course I do, but it has been told by our ancestors that if anyone goes to school from our lineage, they will face death and nothing less," replied her mother with a voice filled with trepidation.

"Let me help, my dear lady," Mr. Thomas cut in. "The word 'school' means a place where you learn new things and the word 'study' means the way you learn new things. If you want your daughter to do greater things in life, you have to send her to the school to learn new things."

That left Latha in deep thought. "Okay, I will let my sweet little Chinni come along to your palace-school," she said.

Chinni was more than delighted and felt a sigh of relief on getting an approval from her mother. She never knew that her dream of being in a palace would come true this way.

Author's note

We are so blessed to have enough money and resources to go to school. Going to school is important for us to enhance our abilities and capabilities and learn to read, write, and solve mathematical problems. So, rain or shine, don't miss school!

Also, do you know that God fulfills the desires of our heart? And in His time, He makes all things beautiful. So, have faith and hold on, no matter what comes your way!

Chapter 9

Princess Chinni goes to school

On the first day of school Chinni woke up as early as she could, to get ready for school. The postman had delivered her school uniform and her school books and bag the other day so now she was on turbo-speed to get ready for school. She first went to the well where she had a bath and brushed her teeth. Next she changed into her uniform which consisted

of a shirt, a pinafore, leggings, socks and shoes. She put them on with much enthusiasm and hurried to the kitchen to make herself a quick breakfast.

Her father was working in the kitchen on a chulha - an earthen stove that was used for cooking on coal or wood fire. She knew how to handle fire, so her father allowed her to assist him, after initial hesitation as she was already dressed for school. There was a large cauldron, blackened by the soot, on top of the fire. Into the cauldron went some oil, coconut milk, pieces of potatoes, onions, green chilies, some curry leaves that were floating like rudderless boats, a few finely chopped ginger and garlic pieces and some salt to taste. That was to serve her family their breakfast along with rotis. For Chinni, this was to be her lunch as well.

And it all got stirred up with a spoon. Next Chinni took a small empty glass jar and poured the stew inside to the brim, sealed it tight and put it into her bag. Whatever stew remained on the wall of the jar was all finished by Chinni in a lickety-split, before she packed it. Then she went to the well and drew water and filled up the bottle for school.

Then she used sand and water to put out the fire and cleaned the cauldron and grill. Now Latha woke up and seeing Chinni all ready and full-stomached, she hugged her responsible daughter and dropped her off at the school-bus stop. As soon as Chinni got on the bus she was surrounded by shouts of joy and laughter as well as bored chatter alike from students from all around the world! There was only one vacant seat left so Chinni quickly and happily took it.

As they reached near the school, the bus became quiet. Chinni watched meekly as the bus drew closer to the school and it was soon seen in full view. Anyone would have thought that a great Indian Maharajah lived in Chinni's new school as from outside the school really looked like the grand palace that Chinni had dreamed of often. But it was a quiet place to study, once you entered.

The bus finally stopped in the parking bay and the whole lot tumbled out, exhausted from the long ride. They looked so tired that anyone would have thought that they travelled all the way from Jammu and Kashmir to Sri Lanka.

Very soon Chinni saw the big main entrance which was decorated with large artificial gems, jewels and precious metals. Chinni didn't know that they were artificial and she was in awe of the décor and cautiously stepped in through the door. She soon found her classroom and took a seat and settled down. There were 30 students in her class in all (including her). Fifteen were girls and 15 were boys, fairly balanced. Soon after, Chinni's classmates entered, all of them carrying fancy bags and fancy things.

After the lesson was over and it was break time, all the children started talking to each other and having their snacks. A gang of three girls and three boys came over to her and when they found out about her meek background, they made fun of her and told the whole class about it in a mocking manner.

This made Chinni feel sad. At home she could always run away to a corner and weep as long as she wanted to, and it calmed her and gave her relief. But here that would be a babyish act, but still she couldn't stop herself from shedding a few tears.

The teacher was furious when she walked inside the classroom and found Chinni crying and after inquiring the matter found out who was responsible for making Chinni cry. She counseled Chinni and the class children and told them that everyone deserves respect irrespective of their background. She told them about A.P.J. Abdul Kalam who was a prominent Indian scientist who also served as the 11th President of India. "Even though the family was not financially well-off, the children were raised in an atmosphere filled with love. He was a very good student and was always curious to learn more about how things happened," she said. "We all need to be like Mr. Kalam, focusing on what is important to gain, the knowledge and progress in life," she added.

Soon after, the children apologised to Chinni. She made new friends and her friends fondly nicknamed her a "Princess Chinni". She settled down to the life of a school girl and lived happily.

From that day onwards Chinni would never have to be bored again for she would go to her school in her grand little school bus.

"Amma, it's already 7:45 am may I go outside and check if my school bus has arrived?" She would ask every day.

She even made up a poem about school,

Oh, I love school,
I love school it's nice,
as nice as it can be...

Rain or sun or snow or mist
I'll be there, it's my plea

Oh, I love school, I love school
it's nice, as nice as it can be, yeah!

Author's note

Don't judge others for their appearances or backgrounds. Respect one and all for who they are. The best act of kindness that you could show at school, is to make friends with someone who is being left out. Don't let anyone bully you or your friends at any point of time. We go to school to learn new things and progress! Have fun at school and treasure those memories.

Notes

Notes

Notes

Notes

Notes